COLA 2024:

Understanding the Cost-of-Living Adjustment for Social Security Benefits

By

Clifford M. Brooks

TABLE OF CONTENTS

INTRODUCTION TO COLA

The annual adjustment given to salaries, pensions, or benefits to reflect changes in the cost of living is known as a cost-of-living adjustment, or COLA. It is intended to mitigate the consequences of inflation and make sure that over time, people's purchasing power is largely steady.

The Consumer Price Index (CPI), which calculates the average change in prices for a basket of goods and services over time, serves as the standard foundation for COLA. The COLA percentage is calculated by using the CPI to compute the rate of inflation.

The goal of COLA is to shield people from the debilitating impacts of inflation. If COLA didn't exist, fixed incomes like pensions and social security payouts would eventually lose their ability to keep up with rising costs. COLA aids people in maintaining their level of living by altering these salaries in response to changes in the cost of living.

The economy as a whole and individuals may both be significantly impacted by COLA. For seniors, COLA makes sure that their pensions increase in line with inflation, enabling them to pay for necessities like housing, healthcare, and food. Knowing that their pay would be modified to reflect the changing cost of living might provide employees with a sense of stability.

From an economic perspective, COLA provides advantages as well as possible disadvantages. Positively, COLA might encourage consumer spending and economic expansion. People are more likely to spend money on goods and services when they have more purchasing power as a result of higher incomes, which can increase economic activity and employment.

COLA, though, can also be difficult. Offering COLA to employees raises labor costs for firms, which may affect their profitability and capacity to compete. Additionally, people may still see a decline in their purchasing power if the rate of inflation is higher than the COLA adjustment.

COLA is frequently used by governmental organizations, including Social Security administrations, pension funds, and labor unions, to calculate annual adjustments to benefits or pay. Depending on the company or nation, many methods might be used to calculate COLA. Others take into account other elements like productivity growth or regional variances in the cost of living, while some utilize a fixed percentage based on the CPI.

It's crucial to remember that COLA is not always applied; the presence and scope of the policy can change between various nations and organizations. In some circumstances, alternative methods—such as negotiated pay raises—might be utilized in place of or in addition to COLA.

In general, COLA is essential for reducing the effects of inflation on people's salaries and preserving their purchasing power. COLA serves to guarantee that people can pay for their basic needs and maintain their level of life over time by modifying salaries, pensions, or benefits depending on increases in the cost of living. However, depending on the particular situation and application, COLA's efficacy and ramifications can change.

WHAT IS COLA IN CHAPTER 1?

COLA, or Cost-of-Living Adjustment, is an acronym. To help beneficiaries keep up with inflation, Social Security payouts are increased yearly. The Consumer Price Index for Urban Wage Earners and Clerical Workers (CPI-W), which gauges the average change in prices paid by urban consumers for a sample basket of goods and services, serves as the foundation for COLA.

1.1 Why is it Important?

It's crucial to comprehend the cost-of-living adjustment (COLA) for Social Security benefits for several reasons.

1. Financial planning: Individuals and families can make better financial plans by understanding how the COLA affects Social Security benefits. They can budget

appropriately, taking into account the rising cost of living, by being able to predict their future income.

2. Planning for retirement: Social Security benefits frequently make up a sizable amount of retirement income. Retirees can anticipate and evaluate how inflation will affect their income throughout retirement years if they are aware of the COLA.

3. Senior advocacy: By being aware of the COLA, seniors and their advocates are better equipped to keep informed and participate in conversations about prospective modifications or changes to the Social Security system. They can then argue for COLA estimates that fairly account for the increased cost of necessities.

4. COLA adjustments have a wider range of economic ramifications. To evaluate how well the system supports retirees and contributes to the general economy, it is helpful to understand how these adjustments are made and how they affect seniors' purchasing power.

5. Social equity: By supporting seniors in keeping up with the rising cost of essential goods and services, the COLA helps to maintain social equality. It is possible to fairly evaluate the COLA's contribution to lowering senior disparity by having a thorough understanding of it.

Overall, it's critical to comprehend the cost-of-living adjustment for Social Security payments if you want to plan your finances wisely, prepare for retirement, advocate for seniors, comprehend how it affects the economy, and encourage social equality among retirees.

1.2 The Origins of COLA

Since its initial implementation in 1975, COLA has been added to Social Security benefits annually. Depending on the rate of inflation, the COLA's amount changes every year. The COLA has varied greatly over the years, reaching as high as 14.3% in some years and as low as 0% in others.

The concept of Cost-of-Living Adjustment (COLA) dates back to the 20th century and was developed in response to the difficulties that people encountered financially during periods of severe inflation. Here is a synopsis of COLA's past:

1930s–1940s: During the Great Depression and World War II, there was considerable economic unrest and a rise in living expenses. In response, several labor unions put "escalator clauses" into wage agreements, which permitted compensation increases based on fluctuations in the cost of living.

In 1952, the Social Security Act Amendments, which were passed by the US Congress, established the idea of COLA. As a result of changes in the Consumer Price Index, automatic benefit increases were provided by this legislation.

1960s: As American inflation started to increase, COLA received more attention. President John F. Kennedy issued an executive order in 1962 inserting a COLA mechanism into salary adjustments for federal employees.

1972: COLA became a key component in preserving the American Social Security benefits' ability to be spent. The CPI-W, or Consumer Price Index for Urban Wage Earners and Clerical Workers, is the index that legislation uses to determine Social Security COLA payments. This connected the changes to the inflation that urban wage earners and office workers experienced.

Late 1970s to early 1980s: High inflation rates were seen during this period as a result of oil price shocks and other economic issues. During this time, COLA became more and more crucial to safeguard people on fixed incomes from the decline in their purchasing power.

The 1990s–2000s: To better combat inflation, the US and other nations kept improving their COLA programs. To guarantee more precise and timely adjustments, changes were made to the calculating processes and frequency of modifications.

Today: COLA is still a widely used practice in many nations and organizations, with annual adjustments being the norm. However, different legal systems use different computations and specialized processes.

Over time, COLA has developed into a crucial component in preserving peoples' standard of living and financial security. It offers a way to counteract the impacts of inflation and guarantee that benefits, pensions, and wages stay up with the rising cost of living.

1.3 The significance of COLA for beneficiaries of Social Security

Because it ensures that beneficiaries' benefits increase at a rate that keeps up with the rising cost of living, COLA is a crucial component of the Social Security program. Beneficiaries' purchasing power would gradually decrease in the absence of COLA since prices for goods and services would rise as a result of inflation.

For low-income recipients, who are more likely to spend a bigger percentage of their income on needs like food and shelter, COLA is particularly crucial. COLA assists in preserving the standard of living for Social Security beneficiaries by assisting in reducing the effects of inflation.

For Social Security beneficiaries, the Cost-of-Living Adjustment (COLA) is crucial. For those people, COLA is essential for the following reasons:

Keep Your Purchasing Power: Over time, COLA aids retirees and other Social Security recipients in keeping their purchasing power. A fixed income loses value as prices for goods and services rise as a result of inflation. Benefit recipients can maintain their level of living and be able to buy necessities thanks to COLA, which enables Social Security benefits to keep pace with the cost of living.

Offset Inflationary Effects: As money's value declines due to inflation, prices rise. Social Security benefits would remain constant and progressively lose their purchasing power absent COLA. By offering consistent increases correlated with changes in the Consumer Price Index, COLA adjustments seek to mitigate the effects of inflation.

Cover Increasing Healthcare Costs: Healthcare costs typically increase more quickly than the rate of ordinary inflation. Beneficiaries of Social Security are assisted by COLA adjustments in managing rising costs for prescription medications, medical care, and health insurance premiums. Beneficiaries would have trouble affording essential medical services without COLA.

Boost Financial Security: For beneficiaries of Social Security, COLA offers some degree of financial security.

Individuals are better able to plan and budget when they are aware that their benefits will be modified annually to reflect changes in the cost of living. They are better able to plan and fulfill their financial commitments, such as those related to housing, utilities, food, and other necessary expenses.

Reduce the Risk of Poverty: For many retirees and people with disabilities, Social Security benefits provide a crucial safety net. COLA adjustments reduce the likelihood that beneficiaries may experience poverty or financial hardship. By maintaining benefits in line with inflation, COLA offers some protection from the increase in living expenses.

Supports Economic Stimulation: COLA hikes may benefit the overall economy. Beneficiaries of Social Security have more disposable income to spend on goods and services when their benefit payments increase as a result of COLA changes. This increased spending can assist businesses, jobs, and overall economic growth by boosting economic activity.

Promote Social Security's Goals: The Social Security program aims to give retired workers, those with disabilities, and their dependents a dependable source of income. By ensuring that Social Security benefits stay up with the rising cost of living, COLA is essential in achieving this goal. It supports the integrity and efficiency of the system in helping individuals in need of financial assistance.

In conclusion, COLA is crucial for beneficiaries of Social Security. It supports the overall goals of the Social Security system by preserving their purchasing power, reducing the effects of inflation, paying for healthcare expenses, fostering financial stability, lowering the danger of poverty, stimulating the economy, and promoting financial stability.

THE ROLE OF THE CONSUMER PRICE INDEX (CPI) IN DETERMINING THE COLA IS DISCUSSED IN CHAPTER 2.

The Cost-of-Living Adjustment (COLA) for Social Security claimants is heavily influenced by the Consumer Price Index (CPI). The CPI estimates the average change in prices paid by urban consumers for a representative basket of goods and services and is a crucial economic indicator. A variety of commodities, including food, lodging, transportation, clothing, medical care, and entertainment, are included in this basket.

A government organization tasked with monitoring economic data, the Bureau of Labour Statistics (BLS), calculates and publishes the CPI every month. To create the CPI, the BLS gathers price data from tens of thousands of retailers and service providers around the nation. The overall inflation rate, which accounts for changes in consumer costs of living, is then calculated using the index.

The yearly COLA for Social Security is calculated using the CPI-W, a particular variation of the CPI that focuses on urban wage earners and clerical workers. Because it captures the spending habits of people who are more likely to rely on Social Security benefits as their main source of income, the CPI-W is thought to be a suitable indicator for this usage.

The average CPI-W for the third quarter of the current year is compared to the third quarter of the previous year's average CPI-W to calculate COLA. The COLA is calculated as a percentage of the index's change, which indicates growing costs. Then, to account for inflation, this percentage is added to Social Security income.

To preserve the purchasing power of Social Security benefits over time, the CPI is essential. The Social Security Administration wants to shield beneficiaries from the degradation of their payments brought on by inflation by coupling COLA to the CPI-W. For people who depend on Social Security as a major source of income, this aids in preserving a constant quality of life.

2.1 COLA is calculated using CPI-W.

The Consumer Price Index for Urban Wage Earners and Clerical Workers (CPI-W) serves as the foundation for the Cost-of-Living Adjustment (COLA) formula used to determine Social Security benefits. For a representative basket of goods and services, urban consumers' average price changes are tracked by the CPI-W.

The average CPI-W for the third quarter of the current year is compared to the average CPI-W for the third quarter of the preceding year by the Social Security Administration (SSA) to calculate the COLA. The COLA is calculated as a percentage of the index's change, which indicates growing costs. Then, to account for inflation, this percentage is added to Social Security income.

The COLA calculation formula is as follows:

COLA is calculated as [Avg CPI-W Q3 current year - Avg CPI-W Q3 previous year] times 100.

The COLA would be computed as follows, for instance, if the average CPI-W for the third quarter of the current year is 240 and the average CPI-W for the third quarter of the prior year is 230.

COLA = [(240 - 230) / 230] x 100 = 4.35%

To reflect the increase in inflation, Social Security payouts would rise by 4.35% the next year. Because it captures the spending habits of people who are more likely to rely on Social Security payments as their main source of income, the CPI-W is seen as a suitable indicator for calculating COLA. The SSA wants to guarantee that beneficiaries' purchasing power remains constant despite rising prices, hence it bases benefit adjustments on the CPI-W.

Three key processes are commonly included in the calculation of the cost-of-living adjustment (COLA) based on the Consumer Price Index for Urban Wage Earners and Clerical Workers (CPI-W):

The reference period is the time frame used to compare the most recent CPI-W to the most recent CPI-W to compute the COLA. The third quarter of the current year in comparison to the third quarter of the prior year is often the reference period.

The CPI-W index for the reference periods is subtracted from and then divided by the CPI-W index from the reference period from the prior year to calculate the percentage change in CPI-W. The value is then converted to a percentage by multiplying it by 100.

CPI-W change as a percentage equals [(CPI-W current - CPI-W previous) / CPI-W prior] x 100.

Step 3: Calculate the COLA percentage: To determine the COLA increase, the base benefit amount is multiplied by the percentage change in the CPI-W. The monthly benefit payment the person received during the previous year constitutes the basic benefit amount.

Base benefit amount x (CPI-W percentage change divided by 100) equals COLA increase.

For instance, if the base benefit amount is $1,500 per month and the CPI-W change is determined to be 3%, the calculation would be as follows:

COLA increase: $1,500 times (3/100) to equal $45

In this case, the COLA increase would be $45, which would result in a reduction of the individual's monthly payment to $1,545 to reflect the increases in the cost of living.

It's crucial to remember that different nations or organizations may have different procedures and formulas for COLA based on CPI-W. The final COLA computation may also be impacted by additional factors, like as statutory provisions or legislative changes.

2.2 Economic influences on COLA

Social Security benefits' Cost-of-Living Adjustment (COLA) is directly impacted by several economic variables that affect the rate of inflation as a whole. These elements may result in the COLA increasing, decreasing, or even staying the same from year to year.

1. The Consumer Price Index for Urban Wage Earners and Clerical Workers (CPI-W), which measures general inflation, is the main factor impacting COLA. The COLA is raised to help recipients preserve their spending power when inflation increases since the price of goods and services also rises. In contrast, the COLA may be lower or even zero if inflation is low or even negative.

2. Energy Prices: Changes in energy costs, especially those of oil and petrol, can have a big impact on the CPI-W and, as a result, the COLA. Transportation, utility, and other products and services can all increase in price due to rising energy expenses, which would result in a higher COLA. On the other hand, if energy prices drop, the COLA might be less.

3. Food Prices: As a considerable component of household spending, food prices have a significant impact on the CPI-W. An increase in food costs may result in a greater COLA. However, the effect on COLA can be less significant if food prices remain constant or drop.

4. Economic Development: The state of the economy as a whole can have an impact on COLA. Strong economic conditions and rapid growth may result in greater salaries and a rise in consumer demand for goods and services, which could raise inflation and the COLA. On

the other hand, a slower-growing and weaker economy can lead to lower inflation and a smaller COLA.

5. Decisions made by the Federal Reserve on its monetary policy may have an indirect impact on COLA. When the Fed increases interest rates to fight inflation, it may delay economic expansion and lessen inflationary pressures, which may result in a smaller COLA. On the other hand, lowering interest rates by the Fed to boost the economy could result in higher inflation and a bigger COLA.

In conclusion, the COLA is a dynamic adjustment that takes into account the shifting economic environment. The Social Security Administration works to guarantee that recipients' benefits keep up with inflation and retain their purchasing power over time by taking into account a variety of economic factors.

CHAPTER 3: COLA 2024 PROJECTIONS AND ESTIMATES: EARLY PROJECTIONS FOR COLA 2024

According to early predictions, COLA 2024 will see a hike of about 3.2%. This estimate is based on data from the Consumer Price Index for Urban Wage Earners and Clerical Workers (CPI-W), which indicated an average increase of 3.2% compared to the same period in 2022 for the first two months of the third quarter of 2023. The Social Security Administration (SSA), following the announcement of the CPI-W data for September 2023, will issue the final COLA for 2024 in October 2023.

Early estimates, however, indicate that beneficiaries would have a minor boost in their benefits in 2024 after experiencing a historically high COLA of 8.7% in 2023. The direction of inflation, energy prices, and economic growth are just a few of the variables that may have an impact on the final COLA for 2024. The COLA may be a little less than 3.2% if inflation remains mild. The COLA can be larger if inflation unexpectedly picks up speed.

For Social Security seniors, the anticipated 3.2% COLA for 2024 would be a sizable raise, giving them extra money to help offset growing living expenses. Beneficiaries who rely on Social Security as their only source of income would see some respite from the boost, even though it might not completely balance the effects of inflation.

3.1 Elements that could affect the possible growth

The likelihood of a COLA hike in 2024 may depend on several factors, including:

Consumer Price Index for Urban Wage Earners and Clerical Workers (CPI-W), which measures general inflation, is the main factor in determining COLA. The COLA may be a little less than 3.2% if inflation remains mild. The COLA can be larger if inflation unexpectedly picks up speed.

Energy Prices: Changes in energy costs, especially those of oil and petrol, can have a big impact on the CPI-W and, as a result, the COLA. The COLA can be lower if energy costs drop or remain flat. The COLA might be larger, though, if oil costs rise as a result of geopolitical developments or supply interruptions.

Food Prices: The CPI-W heavily depends on food prices, and the trajectory of these prices might affect the COLA. The effect on COLA could not be as significant if food prices drop or remain flat. However, it may result in a higher COLA if food costs rise as a result of unfavorable weather or supply-chain interruptions.

Economic Development: COLA may be indirectly impacted by the economy's general health. If the economy continues to expand strongly, higher incomes and a rise in demand for goods and services might raise inflation and the COLA. However, if global economic uncertainty or rising interest rates cause economic growth to stagnate, this might lead to lower inflation and a smaller COLA.

Decisions made by the Federal Reserve regarding its monetary policy may also indirectly affect COLA. If the Fed keeps raising interest rates to fight inflation, it would slow economic expansion and lessen inflationary pressures, which might result in a smaller COLA in the future. However, if the Fed delays or stops raising rates because it is worried about economic growth, it may allow inflation to continue, which might lead to a higher COLA.

3.2 Comprehending how COLA affects benefits

A key factor in ensuring that Social Security benefits retain their purchasing power over time is the Cost-of-Living Adjustment (COLA). Beneficiaries must comprehend how COLA affects benefits to correctly plan their money and decide on their retirement security.

1. Preserving Purchasing Power: By adjusting Social Security benefits for inflation, COLA serves to safeguard the benefits' purchasing power. This means that beneficiaries receive a commensurate increase in their benefits to assist them in maintaining their level of living as the cost of goods and services rises.

2. Offsetting Inflationary Effects: As a result of inflation, money loses value over time and today's dollar is worth less than it did in the past. By raising benefits to keep pace with increased living expenses, COLA helps to counteract this effect. This makes sure that beneficiaries

can still afford necessities like food, housing, and medical care.

3. Effect on Monthly Payments: All Social Security payments, such as retirement, disability, and survivor benefits, are subject to COLA. A proportion of the beneficiary's current benefit sum is used to determine the increase. For instance, if the beneficiary's current monthly benefit is $1,000 and the COLA is 3%, their benefit will rise by $30, making their new monthly benefit $1,030.

4. Compounding Effect: COLA increases have a compounding effect over time, which means that each year's gain builds on the increase from the year before. In the long run, this ensures that benefits keep up with inflation, giving beneficiaries a more steady source of income.

5. Importance for Low-Income Beneficiaries: Low-Income Beneficiaries who largely rely on Social Security as their main source of income are especially in

need of COLA. The yearly increment aids in maintaining their purchasing power and their capacity to pay for the needs of life.

To make wise financial decisions and prepare for a safe retirement, Social Security beneficiaries must comprehend how COLA may affect their benefits. For low-income beneficiaries in particular, COLA offers a more reliable source of income while also assisting in maintaining the purchasing power of benefits.

CHAPTER 4: IMPACT OF COLA ON SOCIAL SECURITY BENEFICIARIES: EFFECTS OF COLA ON MONTHLY BENEFITS

Monthly Social Security benefits are directly impacted by the Cost-of-Living Adjustment (COLA), which raises them to reflect growing inflation. Beneficiaries can continue to afford necessary goods and services despite price increases thanks to this modification.

A percentage of the beneficiary's existing benefit amount is used to determine the COLA. For instance, if the COLA is 3% and a person now receives $1,000 per month in benefits, their benefit will rise by $30, or $100, to become $1,030 per month.

All Social Security benefits, including retirement, disability, and survivor benefits, are subject to the COLA.

This guarantees that all beneficiaries get the change they require to keep their quality of living.

For low-income beneficiaries who significantly rely on Social Security as their main source of income, the impact of COLA on monthly benefits is particularly significant. They can continue to afford necessities like food, housing, and healthcare thanks to the annual rise, which helps them keep up with escalating prices. Over time, COLA changes have a compounding impact, which means that each year's gain builds on the increase from the year before. In the long run, this ensures that benefits keep up with inflation, giving beneficiaries a more steady source of income.

In short, COLA is essential for preserving the value of Social Security benefits and making sure that beneficiaries can maintain their quality of living in the face of growing inflation.

4.1 Effects on Various Beneficiary Groups

Different beneficiary categories within the Social Security system are affected differently by the Cost-of-Living Adjustment (COLA), reflecting their particular circumstances and reliance on payments.

1. Low-Income Beneficiaries: COLA is vital for low-income beneficiaries who significantly rely on Social Security as their main source of income to retain their purchasing power and be able to afford necessities like food, shelter, and healthcare. They can maintain a minimal level of living and keep up with rising costs thanks to the annual increase.

2. Retirees: Retirees rely on COLA to boost their retirement income and counteract the effects of inflation, especially those with little savings or fixed incomes. The boost enables individuals to keep their purchasing power and pay for necessities without using all of their savings.

3. Disabled Beneficiaries: Costs for medical treatment and living assistance are frequently greater for disabled beneficiaries. Despite growing inflation, COLA enables

them to continue being able to pay for these expenses and live reasonably.

4. Survivor Beneficiaries: Survivor beneficiaries rely on COLA to maintain their financial security and make up for the loss of the principal earner's income. These individuals receive benefits based on the work history of a deceased spouse or parent. The rise enables them to cover recurring costs and keep up their current standard of living.

5. Dual-Eligible Beneficiaries: People who are eligible for both Social Security and Medicare frequently have high medical expenses. They can preserve access to essential healthcare services and keep up with escalating medical costs because of COLA.

In conclusion, COLA is essential for maintaining the value of Social Security benefits and making sure that beneficiaries can maintain their level of living even in the face of growing inflation. For vulnerable populations like low-income beneficiaries, seniors, disabled people, survivors, and dual-eligible beneficiaries, the impact is especially important.

4.2 Addressing the issue of increased living expenses

It might be difficult for Social Security recipients, especially those on fixed incomes or with limited resources, to address concerns about growing living costs. Although the Cost-of-Living Adjustment (COLA) lessens some of the effects of inflation, there are still other methods that may be used to control spending and preserve financial security.

Creating a thorough budget and keeping track of expenses will help you find areas where spending can be cut back or changed. Place a higher priority on necessities like shelter, food, and healthcare, and think about reducing your discretionary spending.

Investigate government assistance programs including food stamps, housing subsidies, and Supplemental Security Income (SSI), which can offer extra financial aid on top of Social Security income.

Investigating Alternative Income Sources: To make extra money, look into side jobs, freelancing, or commercializing interests. Even a small bonus can lessen financial stress and counteract rising prices.

Downsizing and Lifestyle Modifications: To cut costs, think about moving into a smaller, more economical home or changing your lifestyle. This can entail avoiding unnecessary purchases, cooking at home, and taking public transit.

Consult a financial advisor or counselor to create a personalized plan for controlling spending, maximizing benefits, and making wise financial decisions in light of growing living costs.

Using Community Resources: Take advantage of community resources that provide low-cost meals, social activities, and other forms of support, such as food banks, senior centers, and discount programs.

Making Informed Decisions and Advocating for Policies That Support Social Security Beneficiaries' Well-Being: Staying Informed and Engaged requires staying up to date on trends in inflation, governmental initiatives, and future benefit adjustments.

Keep in mind that combating rising living expenses necessitates a multifaceted strategy that combines financial tactics, way-of-life changes, and the use of available resources. Beneficiaries can better manage their finances and keep up a steady quality of living by being proactive and asking for help when they need it.

CHAPTER 5: PLANNING FOR FUTURE COLA ADJUSTMENTS: STRATEGIES FOR MANAGING PERSONAL FINANCES WITH COLA

It takes a combination of proactive tactics and well-informed decision-making to effectively manage personal finances with Cost-of-life Adjustment (COLA) to achieve financial stability and maintain a respectable level of life. The following are some essential strategies to consider:

Establish and Monitor a Budget: Create a thorough budget that lists all of your monthly income and outgoing costs, including those for necessities like housing, food, utilities, and medical care. Keep tabs on your expenditures to find areas where you can cut back or change your expenses.

Focus on meeting vital needs first, making sure you have enough money to pay for housing, food, and medical care. Reduce your expenditure on non-essential items, entertainment, dining out, and other discretionary items.

Investigate Eligibility for Government Assistance Programmes: Look into your eligibility for government assistance programs like food stamps, housing subsidies, and Supplemental Security Income (SSI). The financial assistance offered by these programs can be used in addition to your Social Security income.

Examine Alternative Income Sources: Look into ways to get extra money, such as working part-time, freelancing, or turning a hobby into a business. Even a small bonus can lessen financial stress and counteract rising prices.

Examine Lifestyle Modifications: To cut costs, think about downsizing to a less-expensive home or altering your lifestyle. This can entail minimizing non-essential purchases, taking public transit, and cooking more frequently at home.

Seek Financial Counseling: Speak with a financial expert or counselor to create a specialized plan for handling your money, making the most of your benefits, and making wise financial decisions in light of increased living expenses.

Use Community Resources: Take advantage of community resources that provide low-cost meals, social activities, and other forms of support, such as food banks, senior centers, and discount programs.

Keep Up to Date on Inflation Trends, Government Policies, and Potential Benefit Changes to Make Informed Decisions and Advocate for Policies That Support Social Security Beneficiaries' Well-Being Stay Informed and Active: Stay Involved.

Keep in mind that managing personal finances with COLA necessitates a proactive strategy that incorporates monetary tactics, lifestyle modifications, and the effective use of available resources. You may better manage your finances and maintain a consistent standard of life despite growing costs by following these steps and asking for help when necessary.

5.1 Recognising how COLA will affect retirement planning in the long run

For people to make wise financial decisions and ensure their future well-being, they must understand the long-term effects of Cost-of-Living Adjustment (COLA) on retirement planning. The purchasing power of Social Security benefits, which are sometimes a crucial source of income for retirees, is maintained in large part because of COLA.

1. Preserving Purchasing Power: Over time, COLA contributes to the protection of Social Security benefits' purchasing power, ensuring that retirees may continue to afford basic goods and services despite growing inflation. This maintains their standard of living and lowers their vulnerability to future financial distress.

2. Offsetting Inflationary Effects: As a result of inflation, money loses value over time and will be worth less in the future. By raising benefits to keep pace with increased living expenses, COLA helps to counteract this effect. By doing this, retiree benefits are guaranteed to keep up with inflation and sustain their long-term purchasing power.

3. Impact on Retirement Funds: By changing the sufficiency of retirement funds, COLA may have an impact on retirement planning. Retirees may need to increase their savings if COLA routinely outpaces investment gains to maintain their preferred level of living in retirement.

4. Planning for Uncertainty: Although COLA helps to reduce inflation, it is important to take into account the possibility of unforeseen inflationary spikes or times when COLA is low or nonexistent. To ensure financial stability throughout retirement, retirement plans should include backup plans for these possibilities.

5. Increasing Retirement Income Diversification: Relying only on Social Security benefits may not be enough to provide a comfortable retirement. It is possible to increase financial security and lessen reliance on COLA alone by diversifying retirement income sources, such as personal savings, pensions, or part-time employment.

In conclusion, for making wise financial decisions and ensuring a secure future, it is crucial to comprehend the long-term effects of COLA on retirement planning. To achieve a pleasant retirement, it's important to take into account COLA's influence on savings, plan for risks, and diversify income sources. The purchase power of Social Security benefits is preserved in part by COLA.

5.2 Seeking financial advice to make wise decisions

To make prudent financial decisions, especially when addressing complex issues like retirement planning, investing strategies, and managing personal finances in the face of increased living expenses, it can be a good idea to seek financial advice. Here are some suggestions to consider while looking for financial advice:

Determine Your Needs: Clearly state your financial objectives, worries, and support needs. This will make it easier for you to locate the proper kind of financial advice and guarantee that it is customized to your unique situation.

Think About Your Options: Examine many possibilities for financial advice, including credit counseling programs, fee-only financial consultants, and financial planners. Choose an option that fits your demands and budget since each one offers varying degrees of experience and services.

Ask for Referrals: Consult with friends, relatives, or coworkers to get suggestions for trustworthy financial planners or advisors. Personal recommendations can offer insightful information about the advisor's knowledge, style, and reliability.

Conduct a comprehensive investigation into any potential advisors or planners. Verify their qualifications, experience, areas of expertise, and any disciplinary proceedings that have been taken against them. To determine their reputation and customer happiness, read internet reviews and testimonies.

To discuss your financial condition, goals, and expectations, set up initial consultations with suitable advisors. Check to see how they communicate, if they are approachable, and if they pay close attention to your problems.

Analyze Fees and Services: Recognise the advisor's services and charge schedule. Inquire about their price structure, what services are covered by their fees, and whether they charge a flat fee or a portion of the assets they manage.

Verify Registration and Credentials: Contact the Securities and Exchange Commission (SEC) or the Financial Industry Regulatory Authority (FINRA) to confirm the advisor's registration and credentials.

Analyze your comfort level with the advisor's personality, communication style, and investment philosophy to determine compatibility. Select a companion who shares your values and risk tolerance and with whom you feel at ease and can trust.

Get a Written Agreement: After choosing an advisor, get a written contract stating the services to be provided, payment terms, and roles and obligations of each party. This guarantees transparency and safeguards your interests.

Monitor Performance: Consult your advisor frequently to discuss the performance of your investments and financial plan. Make sure they respond to your inquiries, worries, and evolving circumstances.

Keep in mind that investing in your financial well-being by getting financial advice. You can receive useful information, make wise decisions, and reach your financial objectives by carefully choosing a knowledgeable and reliable advisor.

CHAPTER 6: IMPACT OF COLA ON RETIREMENT PLANNING

For seniors to be able to maintain their quality of living despite inflation, it is essential to incorporate the cost-of-living adjustment (COLA) into retirement income programs. The following are some strategies for including COLA in retirement income planning:

1. Know how the COLA is calculated by being familiar with the process. It is released yearly and is based on the Consumer Price Index for Urban Wage Earners and Clerical Workers (CPI-W). You can make educated projections if you are aware of the formula and past patterns.

2. Long-term inflation should be taken into account because COLA adjustments attempt to keep up with inflation but may not entirely cover all costs. When

planning a retirement budget, take anticipated increases in housing, healthcare, and other essentials into consideration.

3. With the use of retirement calculators, you may more accurately anticipate your future Social Security income by entering estimated COLA percentages. This enables you to evaluate the impact of inflation on your total retirement income strategy.

4. Be prepared for changing costs: Some costs, such as healthcare, may increase faster than the COLA. This should be taken into account while creating your retirement income plan by setting aside more money or looking into supplemental insurance solutions.

5. Relying entirely on Social Security may not be enough to cover all of your retirement needs, so diversify your income sources. To protect against inflation and any potential restrictions on COLA adjustments, think about diversifying your income sources, such as pensions, retirement savings, and investments.

6. Review and modify your plan regularly because COLA changes can change from year to year. Review and update your retirement income plan regularly to make sure it reflects any changes in your situation or financial goals as well as the most recent COLA percentages.

7. Seek expert advice: Working with a financial advisor can provide you access to their knowledge and experience in integrating COLA into your retirement income strategies. They can assist you in situation analysis, inflation forecasting, and any necessary plan modifications.

You can better prepare for the effects of inflation on your income and create a more secure and sustainable financial future by including COLA in your retirement income strategies.

6.1 Adjusting Investment and Savings Plans for COLA Fluctuations

Your retirement funds must be protected and grown by adjusting savings and investment plans for cost-of-living adjustment (COLA) variations. Here are a strategies to consider:

1. Recognise the effects of inflation: Over time, inflation reduces the purchasing power of your money. It's critical to understand that the COLA might not completely counteract inflation. Keep abreast of past inflation rates and anticipated future trends to determine how they may impact your savings and investing objectives.

2. Contributions to your savings should be increased to account for future COLA changes. Increase the percentage of your salary that you set aside for savings or put more money aside for retirement accounts. This acts as a buffer against the rising expense of living.

3. Diversify your investment portfolio: You can lessen the impact of COLA swings by having a well-diversified investment portfolio. Think about distributing your investments through various asset types, including stocks, bonds, real estate, and commodities. By spreading out the risk, diversification raises the possibility that your investments will keep up with rising prices.

4. Invest in inflation-protected securities: Treasury Inflation-Protected Securities (TIPS) are made to offer inflation protection. Think about incorporating these products within your investing portfolio to help protect your savings from changes in the COLA.

5. Review and modify your investment allocations as necessary to make sure they are in line with your long-term retirement objectives and anticipated COLA increases. Regularly rebalance your portfolio to keep a balance of assets that takes inflation and market conditions into account.

6. Keep up with COLA announcements: Be aware of the yearly COLA announcements for Social Security benefits. You can use this information to predict any changes in your income and modify your investing and savings strategy accordingly.

7. Seek expert guidance: When altering savings and investing plans for COLA variations, working with a financial counselor can be a great help. They may analyze your particular position, gauge your risk tolerance, and suggest investing plans that are in line with your objectives.

Keep in mind that COLA adjustments are a continuous process for savings and investment plans. To stay on pace for a comfortable retirement, review your progress frequently, reevaluate your financial objectives, and make any required adjustments.

6.2 Effective Budgeting with COLA Considerations

Effective budgeting that takes cost-of-living adjustment (COLA) into account is essential for controlling spending and ensuring that your income keeps pace with inflation. The following advice will help you create an effective budget:

1. Track and analyze your spending: Begin by maintaining a record of your monthly outlays and separating them into necessities and luxuries. This can help you see clearly where your money is going and show you where you might be able to make cuts or set priorities.

2. The possible influence of inflation on your critical expenses, such as housing, healthcare, groceries, and transportation, should be taken into account while creating a budget. For these categories, look up historical

inflation rates to get a sense of how much they might rise over time.

3. The COLA changes should be taken into account when estimating your Social Security income. Recognize how the COLA percentages are determined and take that into account when creating your budget. You can more properly predict your future income thanks to this.

4. Make a reserve for unforeseen costs: Create an emergency fund to pay for unforeseen costs like auto repairs, house repairs, or medical crises. Your budgetary plans won't be thrown off by surprises if you have a safety net.

5. Determine your long-term financial objectives, such as retirement savings, debt repayment, or saving for a large purchase, and rank them in order of importance. Set aside some of your money for these objectives, and make monthly modifications to reflect changes in your financial condition and COLA adjustments.

6. Regularly assess your budget and make any adjustments to make sure it reflects your current income, expenses, and COLA considerations. Make the required adjustments to account for any changes in inflation or your changing financial situation.

7. Find ways to cut costs: Look for ways to reduce the cost of living. This can entail haggling over pricing, looking for deals or sales, comparing prices, or locating more affordable options. Small savings might add up and assist you in sticking to your spending plan.

8. Consult a financial professional for advice if you're unsure of how to efficiently budget while taking COLA concerns. They can help you develop a budget that takes inflation and your long-term financial objectives into account and provide personalized guidance based on your particular position.

You may better control your spending, put money away for the future, and make sure that your income is enough to cover your requirements despite rising costs by creating a smart budget that takes COLA into account.

CHAPTER 7: MAINTAINING FINANCIAL SECURITY IN A DYNAMIC ECONOMIC ENVIRONMENT: NAVIGATING COLA IN A CHANGING FINANCIAL LANDSCAPE

In a changing economic climate, ensuring financial stability necessitates proactive planning and flexibility. Here are some tips to help you deal with the unstable economic climate:

1. Create an emergency fund: Creating an emergency fund is essential because it offers a financial safety net in the event of unforeseen expenses or interruptions in income. To hedge against economic uncertainty, try to save at least three to six months' worth of spending.

2. Increase your income diversity because relying on a single source of income exposes you to greater risks.

Investigate several revenue streams, such as side jobs, contract work, or passive sources of income like investments or rental properties. This offers a more secure financial base and acts as a bulwark against economic changes.

3. Ensure that your investment portfolio is well-balanced by diversifying it among other asset types, such as equities, bonds, real estate, and commodities. By spreading out the risk, this lessens the effect of market volatility. Review and modify your investments frequently in light of shifting economic conditions and your risk tolerance.

4. Stay informed and take initiative: It's essential to stay current on market and economic developments to make wise financial decisions. To spot potential risks or opportunities, keep up with news, economic data, and market research.

5. Your financial plan should be reviewed and updated frequently to account for shifting economic conditions

and personal circumstances. Determine your objectives and risk tolerance, then modify your strategy as necessary. If necessary, seek expert financial guidance to make sure your plan continues to be in line with your goals.

6. Control your spending and stick to your budget: In a volatile economic climate, it's critical to be aware of your spending patterns and adhere to your spending budget. Prioritize your expenses depending on your budget and financial objectives, and pay attention to the necessities. Avoid taking on unnecessary debt and look for methods to save costs where you can.

7. Create a flexible career mentality since adaptation is essential in a changing economic climate. To stay competitive in the employment market, maintain your adaptability and always improve your abilities. Take into account learning new skills through certifications or courses that are in line with the needs of developing markets or shifting labor markets.

8. Protect yourself with insurance: To reduce financial risks, you must have enough insurance coverage. To make sure you have the right coverage to safeguard you against unforeseen financial obligations, evaluate your insurance requirements, including those for health, vehicle, homeowner's, and disability insurance.

9. Create a strong professional network by connecting with others in the industry. Doing so will help you access chances and advance your career possibilities. In a fast-paced economic environment, networking may help you stay connected, obtain insightful information, and open doors.

In a changing economic climate, ensuring financial stability necessitates being proactive and adaptable. You may more effectively navigate through unstable economic situations and safeguard your financial security by putting these strategies into practice.

CHAPTER 8: LIST OF TERMS RELATED TO COLA

Here is a glossary of terminology associated with Social Security and the Cost-of-Living Adjustment (COLA):

1. COLA (Cost of Living Adjustment): An annual rise in Social Security benefits designed to counteract the effects of inflation and preserve the benefits' buying power.

2. CPI-W (Consumer Price Index for Urban Wage Earners and Clerical Workers): This inflation indicator analyzes the typical change in prices paid by urban consumers for a selection of goods and services. It is applied to calculate the Social Security benefit's yearly COLA.

3. Inflation: A widespread rise in prices and a gradual loss of money's purchasing power. The value of benefits is diminished by inflation, increasing the cost of goods and services.

4. The capacity of a certain sum of money to purchase products and services. By preserving the purchasing power of Social Security benefits, COLA makes sure that recipients may continue to afford necessities despite growing costs.

5. Social Security: A federal initiative that offers qualified people retirement, disability, and survivor benefits. Current employees' payroll taxes are used to pay for it.

6. Beneficiary: A person who receives Social Security payments, such as pensioners, those with disabilities, and the heirs of workers who have passed away.

7. Fixed Income: A consistent flow of income that is unaffected by inflation. Because Social Security benefits

are seen as a fixed income, recipients are especially susceptible to the effects of price increases.

8. Financial Hardship: A situation in which a person or household struggles to meet fundamental demands because of a lack of resources or income. By adjusting benefits for inflation, COLA aids in preventing hardship for Social Security recipients.

9. Social Safety Net: A group of government initiatives created to offer low-income people, the elderly, and those with disabilities a minimal degree of income support and basic services.

10. Economic security: Refers to a person's or a household's capacity to meet their fundamental needs and sustain a consistent level of living. By giving Social Security claimants a consistent source of income, COLA promotes financial stability.

11. Social equity: A society's equitable and just distribution of resources and opportunities. By

guaranteeing that benefits stay up with inflation and defending the purchasing power of vulnerable groups, COLA supports social fairness.

12. Public Trust: The belief held by the populace that the government is capable of running social programs efficiently. By displaying a dedication to preserving the value of Social Security benefits, COLA increases public trust.

8.1 Supplemental sources for comprehending COLA

Here are some other sites to help you learn more about COLA (Cost of Living Adjustment) and how it affects Social Security benefits:

Social Security Administration (SSA): Comprehensive information regarding COLA, including its calculation, historical COLA rates, and the effect on various types of payments, is available on the Social Security Administration's official website.

AARP: Dedicated to enabling older Americans, AARP provides a lot of information about COLA, including explanations, calculators, and advocacy work to safeguard the purchasing power of benefits.

The National Committee to Preserve Social Security and Medicare (NCPSSM) is a nonpartisan advocacy organization that offers an in-depth study of COLA, its effects on recipients, and legislative recommendations for guaranteeing appropriate benefits.

The non-profit research organization Centre on Budget and Policy Priorities (CBPP) provides an in-depth analysis of COLA and its function in preserving the financial stability of vulnerable populations.

Economic Policy Institute (EPI): The EPI is a non-profit research organization that conducts studies on COLA, its effects on income inequality, and policy recommendations for bolstering the social safety net.

CRS: The nonpartisan Congressional Research Service (CRS) offers reports and analyses on COLA, its historical trends, and its policy consequences.

Social Security Works: Social Security Works is a non-profit advocacy group that runs campaigns to safeguard and increase Social Security benefits as well as resources on COLA and its significance for recipients.

Senior Citizens League (TSCL): The TSCL is a non-profit organization that advocates for seniors and offers information about COLA, how it affects senior citizens and advocacy work being done to ensure retiree benefits are adequate.

AARP Foundation: The AARP Foundation, a nonprofit associated with AARP, provides information about COLA, its effects on low-income seniors, and initiatives to help at-risk groups.

The National Council on Ageing (NCOA), a nonprofit organization devoted to enhancing the lives of older people, offers materials to assist seniors in managing their money as well as details on COLA and its effects on Aging populations.

These websites provide a thorough knowledge of COLA's significance for Social Security beneficiaries and the larger social safety net by offering a variety of viewpoints, analyses, and advocacy initiatives.

8.2 Social Security Administration contact details

The Social Security Administration's (SSA) contact information is provided below:

Toll-Free Phone: 1-800-772-1213 (TTY: 1-800-325-0778) Website: https://www.ssa.gov

Monday through Friday, 8:00 AM to 7:00 PM (local time).

https://secure.ssa.gov/ICON/main.jsp Office Locator Frequently Asked Questions (FAQs): https://www.ssa.gov/faq/ My Social Security Account: https://www.ssa.gov/my/ Social Security for People with Disabilities: https://www.ssa.gov/disability/ Social Security for Retirement: https://www.ssa.gov/retirement/ Social Security Supplemental Security Income (SSI): https://www.ssa.gov/ssi Supplemental Security Income (Survivors Benefits): https://www.ssa.gov/benefits/survivors

CHAPTER 9: CONCLUSION

The importance of COLA for the financial stability of Social Security

By preserving the purchasing power of payments and preserving the program's long-term viability, the Cost-of-Living Adjustment (COLA) is essential in sustaining the financial stability of the Social Security program.

1. Preserving Purchasing Power: By increasing Social Security benefits for inflation, COLA helps to preserve the benefits' purchasing power. This minimizes the danger of financial hardship and dependence on more government help while ensuring that beneficiaries can continue to buy basic products and services despite growing costs.

2. Upholding Beneficiary Trust: By displaying a commitment to shielding beneficiaries' benefits from inflation, COLA upholds beneficiaries' faith in the Social Security program. The public's continuing support of the program and its political viability depends on this confidence.

3. Lessening Financial Stress: By adjusting beneficiaries' payments for inflation, COLA lessens the strain on their finances, especially for those with fixed spending or low incomes. This can lessen the strain on other social programs by preventing poverty among the elderly and disabled.

4. Fostering Economic Stability: By giving millions of Americans a steady stream of income, COLA promotes general economic stability. In times of inflation, this aids in sustaining consumer spending, boosting local economies, and stabilizing the overall economy.

5. Ensuring Long-Term Viability: COLA contributes to the long-term sustainability of the Social Security

program by preserving the buying power of benefits. For the program to continue offering necessary retirement, disability, and survivor benefits to future generations, this is vital.

In conclusion, COLA is an essential part of the Social Security program that ensures recipients' financial security, upholds program credibility, and promotes general economic stability. By preserving the benefits' purchasing power, COLA contributes to ensuring the program's long-term stability and achieving its goal of offering crucial support to millions of Americans.

9.1 Considering COLA Factors When Planning for a Sustainable Financial Future

To ensure that your income stays up with rising costs, it is essential to plan for a healthy financial future that takes cost-of-living adjustment (COLA) factors into account. The following actions will assist you in making plans for a stable financial future:

1. Start by assessing your income, expenses, and overall financial health as you assess your present financial condition. Consider your current assets, liabilities, and any ongoing debt obligations. Your financial planning will have a baseline thanks to this examination.

2. Establish financial objectives: Clearly state your short- and long-term financial objectives. These could include funding education, saving for retirement, clearing debt, or preparing for a down payment on a home. You may create a financial planning roadmap by having clear goals.

3. COLA adjustments should be taken into account when estimating your future income, including Social Security benefits. Do some research on previous COLA percentages, then include them in your estimates. This will make it easier for you to predict your income in the future and make plans accordingly.

4. Develop a reasonable budget in line with your financial objectives and anticipated COLA increases. Make careful to factor inflation into the cost of necessities like housing, healthcare, and transportation. Make sure your budget is reasonable and sustainable while allocating money for savings, debt repayment, and discretionary expenditure.

5. Strategically save and invest: Increase your savings by allocating a portion of your monthly income to savings. Think about making contributions to investment vehicles like 401(k)s, IRAs, or other retirement funds. Your investing portfolio should be diversified to reduce risk and increase possible profits. Review and modify your investing plan regularly in light of market conditions and your risk tolerance.

6. Healthcare costs should be budgeted for because they frequently increase more quickly than the normal rate of inflation. When making your financial strategy, take prospective increases in healthcare expenditures into

account. To help with possible costs, think about starting a health savings account (HSA) or buying long-term care insurance.

7. Strategically pay off debt by putting high-interest debt, such as credit cards or personal loans, at the top of the list. Make a debt payback strategy that works with your spending plan and financial objectives. Less debt means more money available for savings and investments.

8. Continue your education by keeping up with changing financial trends, investing methods, and personal finance topics. Learn about issues like estate planning, tax preparation, and retirement planning. You may make informed decisions and change your financial strategy as necessary with the help of this information.

9. Regularly review and revise your financial plan to make sure it stays in line with your objectives and changing circumstances. Review your spending plan, savings plan, investment holdings, and any modifications

to COLA adjustments. As required, make adjustments to make sure your strategy is still on course for a secure financial future.

10. Seek expert advice: If you're feeling uncertain or overburdened by the thought of making financial plans that take COLA issues into account, you might want to talk to a financial advisor. They may offer you individualized guidance, assist you in analyzing your particular circumstances, and direct you toward making decisions that are in line with your objectives.

You may proactively plan for a financially stable future that takes COLA adjustments into account and ensures your income keeps up with rising costs by following these steps. Keep an eye on your strategy and make adjustments as needed to move towards your financial objectives.

9.2 Making sure recipients receive appropriate benefits, both now and in the future

A multifaceted strategy that tackles both short-term and long-term concerns is necessary to guarantee enough Social Security benefits for present and future beneficiaries. The following are important points to keep in mind:

1. Maintaining the Cost-of-Living Adjustment (COLA): The Cost-of-Living Adjustment (COLA) is necessary for maintaining the purchasing power of benefits and ensuring that beneficiaries can afford basic goods and services. To stop the erosion of benefits owing to inflation, a constant and accurate COLA must be maintained.

2. Addressing Demographic Shifts: Long-term funding of the Social Security system is difficult due to the Aging population and rising proportion of pensioners in comparison to workers. The program's sustainability

might be improved by looking into solutions to demographic shifts, including gradually raising the retirement age or changing contribution rates.

3. Diversifying Funding Sources: Payroll taxes on current employees are the main source of funding for Social Security. Reducing reliance on payroll taxes and ensuring appropriate funding for future beneficiaries could be achieved by diversifying funding sources, such as by taking into account additional revenue sources or investigating alternative financing methods.

4. Improving Benefit Adequacy: Although the COLA helps maintain the purchasing power of benefits, it might not be enough to guarantee that all beneficiaries live up to an adequate standard of living. A more fair distribution of benefits could be achieved by considering potential adjustments to benefit amounts, especially for low-income beneficiaries.

5. Fostering Financial Literacy: Providing present and future beneficiaries with information on financial

planning, retirement savings, and maximizing Social Security payments will help them make wise decisions and ensure their financial security. Increasing financial knowledge might inspire people to plan for their future and lessen their dependence on Social Security alone.

6. Addressing Income disparity: It can be difficult to guarantee sufficient benefits for all recipients while income disparity continues to grow. Reducing the strain on Social Security and ensuring a more equitable distribution of resources can be accomplished by addressing income disparity through policies that support equitable salaries, progressive taxes, and economic opportunity.

7. Maintaining Public Support: Social Security's continued sustainability depends on maintaining public support. Transparent discussion of the program's problems and potential solutions helps build trust and motivate people to adopt policies that provide sufficient benefits for the present and future generations.

A comprehensive strategy that strikes a balance between the requirements of present recipients and the program's long-term viability is necessary to ensure adequate Social Security benefits. Policymakers can protect this crucial program for future generations by addressing demographic changes, diversifying financing sources, improving benefit adequacy, fostering financial literacy, tackling income inequality, and retaining public support.

9.3 Understanding the COLA's contribution to the upkeep of the social safety net

The Cost-of-Living Adjustment (COLA), which preserves the purchasing power of benefits and guarantees that needy populations may afford basic goods and services, is vital to preserving the social safety net.

Protecting Vulnerable Populations: COLA protects the welfare of vulnerable populations, including the elderly, the disabled, and low-income people who heavily rely on Social Security and other government benefits. They can maintain their standard of living and are protected from poverty and other financial hardships thanks to COLA, which adjusts benefits for inflation.

Maintaining Economic Stability: By giving millions of Americans a steady stream of income, COLA helps to maintain general economic stability. This eases the burden on other social programs and supports local economies while stabilizing household finances.

Promoting Social fairness: By ensuring that benefits increase at the same rate as inflation and closing the growing gap between benefit levels and rising living expenses, COLA works to advance social fairness. This ensures that vulnerable persons may retain a respectable standard of living and prevents the loss of benefits.

Financial Hardship Prevention: By adjusting payments for inflation, COLA helps protect beneficiaries from facing financial hardship, especially those with fixed expenses or low incomes. By doing so, you can lessen poverty, rely less on government help, and live happier, healthier lives.

Increasing Public Trust: By displaying a dedication to preserving the worth of benefits and making sure that they continue to be pertinent to beneficiaries' needs, COLA increases public confidence in the social safety net. For social programs to continue to get support from the general population and remain viable, this confidence is essential.

In summary, COLA acts as an essential tool for preserving thc social safety net, shielding populations at risk from the deterioration of their benefits owing to inflation. COLA fosters economic security, social equality, and financial stability for millions of Americans by guaranteeing that benefits stay up with rising costs.

www.ingramcontent.com/pod-product-compliance
Lightning Source LLC
Chambersburg PA
CBHW061000260726
48661CB00005B/1957